EARTH GIANT TREE GIFT SERIES – BOOK 6

Pagoda Tree's Gift

ROCHELLE HEVEREN

 TREE VOICE PUBLISHING

Earth Giant Tree Gift Series: Pagoda Tree's Gift

TREE VOICE PUBLISHING PTY LTD
ACN. 627 784 294 ABN . 94627784294
4 Wirreanda Court Blackburn Victoria 3130 AUSTRALIA
Phone +613 9878 4600
Email: hello@treevoice.global
www.treevoice.global

First published in 2019
Copyright text © Rochelle Heveren
Copyright © Tree Voice Publishing

www.facebook.com/TreeVoiceAuthor
www.facebook.com/RochelleHeverenAuthor
Instagram: @treevoiceglobal
Instagram: @rochelle_with_love_x

All rights reserved. No part of this publication may be reproduced in whole or in part, stored in a retrievable system, or transmitted in any form or by any means, electronic, mechanical, photocopying, recording or otherwise, without written permission of the copyright holder or publisher.

Designed by Tree Voice Publishing Pty Ltd
Printed by Ingram Spark
ISBN: 978-0-6483913-0-2 (paperback)

 A catalogue record for this book is available from the National Library of Australia

*I know with my whole being,
that when I sit and a tree connects,
that it is never just for me.*

*This little book
has BIG heart and soul.*

*My commitment to share this with you,
my friend, is promised.*

– Love Rochelle xxx

Sitting at the base of this wise Pagoda tree in Xi'an China, over two thousand years old, I feel instant calm, clarity, focus and peace. I discover that with a clear mind I can learn more.

Pagoda reminds me of the importance of paying attention to what I focus my thoughts on and how I can clear my mind for focus and clarity. This immediately untangles my mind so I can finally live without this distraction.

Foreword

Pagoda Tree's Gift is the channelled teachings of one of Earth's great Masters. This wise tree, over two thousand years old, will bring you calm, clarity, focus and peace – a unique way of guiding life's journey, reminding you of the importance of calm in all areas of your life. You will discover that with a clear mind you can learn more. Pagoda will remind you of the importance of paying attention to what you focus your thoughts on and how to clear your mind for focus and clarity. Experience deep contemplation, stillness and calm while connecting into Pagoda.

Being supported with the magic of *Pagoda Tree's Gift* is like resting your back against his trunk and listening to his whispers of great wisdom. Allow his words to encourage you with love.

This inspiring gift book is designed to unlock your own heart's wisdom. Rochelle invites you to discover the magic, stillness and newfound clarity that she experienced, sitting and resting her back against the Pagoda tree in Xi'an, China.

Written in Xi'an, China

Contents

Introduction 1

Chapter 1: Meeting Pagoda 4

Chapter 2: Silence 9

Chapter 3: Reaction 13

Chapter 4: Give-Away 'Essence' 18

Chapter 5: Family 22

Chapter 6: Embrace Your Personal Story 26

Chapter 7: Clarity for More 29

Chapter 8: Control 35

Chapter 9: Balance...................................... 40

Chapter 10: State of Mind 44

Chapter 11: My Journey Continues 48

Introduction

Planes, bullet trains, and big and little buses take us into the heart and all across China.

When I arrive in Chengdu, a sense of quiet settles over me that instantly invokes a blissful feeling of calm. I am surprised as I'm in the midst of many skyscrapers. Here in China many live in high-rise buildings.

Around every corner I observe abundant greenery climbing across and around buildings. Plant life bursts from every pot or plot of soil. Up and beneath the layered roadways, vines hug the concrete structures. The lush green hanging vines are stunningly beautiful. In every patch of dirt bursts a tree, plant or group of flowers. Being in China is like being in a massive landscaped garden. I wonder if these cities were designed in this way on purpose to give balance between buildings and nature. I haven't experienced this before in any other major city. I wonder if China has discovered the vital ingredient of balance.

In Chengdu I am taken to see the playful pandas. As a country, China is very proud of the panda. Pandas have distinctive black and white furry coats and appear very loveable and cuddly, yet I'm cautioned about their sharp teeth and claws. When they lived in the wild they ate meat, but now bamboo. I join a large queue that leads to the view of three baby pandas sleeping in a nursery cot. It feels special to connect to the panda. I learn that pandas auspiciously symbolise peace, harmony and friendship.

I walk through the Panda Park and notice that alongside all the pathways there are many bamboo plants. This is convenient as rain is forecast for today. I smile, knowing that nature is providing a natural umbrella.

After the Panda Park we enjoy some of the large sprawling parks scattered around the city. I learn these gardens are the meeting places for friends to catch up, perhaps to watch mini concerts or join in on an upbeat version of Thai Chi.

I sip on my brewed Chinese tea in a far corner of a massive tea house as I sit between trees overlooking the lake. I continue to experience the

Ying Yang balance of China. After my calming cup of tea I wander around to explore more of this garden. Social media is banned here so there isn't any access to the outside world through Facebook, Instagram or Twitter.

Here in this garden, on the opposite side to the tea house, is a corner surrounded by a long picket fence. On the pickets notices and advertisements have been posted by people seeking prospective partners. I find this an interesting alternative to the dating websites back home. Some notices have been posted by parents desperate to find a partner for their handsome son or beautiful daughter. I am amused as I watch people scribbling down the details. There's a busy vibe of excitement. I enjoy watching people do that which they have done for a very long time. This is perhaps more social than what we call 'social media' back home.

The trees in this garden are ancient. I imagine they've become extremely supportive over the many years of living alongside each another. The older trees hold stable space and protection for all the smaller trees beneath – a beautiful example of generations living together.

I feel a sense of welcome, balanced energy and peace.

CHAPTER 1

Meeting Pagoda

Today I visit the *Little Wild Goose Pagoda* in Xi'an. My heart beats faster as I walk around the gardens here.

Instant calm, stillness and deep contemplation blanket me.

My new friend draws me closer. I am almost in a trance meditative state as I near such an old and graceful tree. The central trunk is solid, partly burned, but supported. The beautiful graceful leaves look featherlike and soft. They dance in the gentle breeze.

At first I notice a full grove of Pagoda trees. Then I am taken by a strong feeling as soon as I see my friend. I notice others in this area are also gravitating to this one tree. In awe they admire, take photos, and sit and rest.

"I see you," I say as I walk up and sit at the base of this majestic tree. And what I see is a presence much bigger than my own limited human experience – one who encompasses a full range of being – not restricted to either male or female. But how can that be?

I put my questions aside, as I watch her strong elegant fingertips of soft flowing leaves dance.

"I also see you. Your beauty is my mirror. Hearts unite and minds are calmed. The scholar needed this exact calm before any knowledge could be contained," Pagoda speaks.

I have no words right now. Instead I want to bathe and soak in all these new feelings. Being freed from my tangled mind chatter is such a unique experience for me.

"I feel honoured to meet someone so old and wise," I say eventually.

"And I am thrilled to meet my next student." Pagoda's words excite me about what will come next.

I sit for a long time. I wonder if I am feeling a stillness before a storm. In life I have sometimes felt calm before everything started thrashing in every direction. I let that fear dissipate.

When I rest and connect to a tree, a threading always takes place between us. This creates shifts throughout my life.

I hear the words: "Through the eye of a needle."

I laugh to myself, knowing that these days threading a needle is quite a task as my vision isn't as sharp as it once was. In fact my body has worn down over my 50 years. My attention is drawn to Pagoda. Time affects trees differently than it does humans. Time allows strength – trunks widen and roots reach deep into the earth to hold firm, steadying them to withstand all challenges that arrive. I notice that even though there are burnt parts of Pagoda, that he has survived the fires and still grown. I imagine that wisdom is achieved through a tree's growth and experiences.

"Are you family with the other Pagoda trees here in Xian?" I ask.

"Yes, and we hold hands through our underground root system. Together we are like one." Pagoda confirms my hunch. "It is not just those in this grove that are family, but all the other Pagoda trees here on earth."

"I expect that support and family are so important to live a happy healthy life," I comment.

I think of my own family, my friends and people in community, and understand how I do feel part of something bigger than myself when I am connected to others.

"Together better," I say. Then I pause before offering my next observation: "I bet you have witnessed a rich history here in China."

"Time is history, the story and legend passed down. The knowledge of yesterday feeds the minds of tomorrow," Pagoda responds.

"Do many people touch, admire and connect to you here?" I ask.

"There are some who stop to connect, but there are also many who pass right by."

"Are you ever saddened by this?" I ask.

"Never. I know that my life is not of interest to all. Regardless of the reason for their visit, I know that every mind is always calmed by breathing my air," Pagoda shares this secret.

I smile with recognition. I know a bit about energy and understand it is always at play regardless of people's awareness of this fact.

"I would love to see you in full bloom. I bet you are breathtaking." I imagine what this courtyard grove would look like full of Pagoda tree flowers.

"Just as you are, my friend," Pagoda reflects back at me.

I imagine that I would be beautiful if I were in full bloom as well. Colourful and vibrant, I would be!

Closing my eyes, I embrace the image of tree and woman beside each other. My new friend is such a treasure. Not just to me but to all who sit, walk by or look at his deep bark crevices. The magic of calm threads to all.

"Thank you for my state of mind now calmed," I say.

"Thank you for my heart, full and happy," Pagoda responds.

CHAPTER 2

Silence

I'm eager for my first lesson to begin with my teacher, the Pagoda tree, who has waited patiently for his new scholar.

Conveniently there's a square timber seat built around Pagoda. I sit comfortably and wait until I am spoken to. This is unusual for me – I usually bound on in and speak first.

After only a short time, Pagoda opens the conversation: "You've displayed patience in your ability for silence. I'm impressed that you haven't needed to be told to do this."

"As soon as I'm near you, I feel not only silence in my mind, I also feel like not talking... well, conversation is different if I'm spoken to. I don't feel like my usual chatty self!" I smile as I respond. "This is good. Speak only when spoken to."

I observe people around me walking up to admire my friend without speaking. I wonder if silence is one of his gifts. I wonder if this silence was one of the principles taught here well over two thousand years ago. I remember being told that the *Little Wild Goose Pagoda* was a place of monks. The Buddhists gathered to be silent and learn.

I had my own experience with noble silence when I attended Vipassana many years ago. There I was taught through many hours of sitting in silent noble meditation. I could sit for hours without moving my body, and my mind also became still. During that week every activity like eating, sleeping, dressing, meditating – even brushing my teeth – was carried out with a clear, calm mind.

"Noble silence is a gift," Pagoda begins. "Only when your outer world becomes quiet, followed by your inner calm, can you really learn."

"My many tumbled thoughts have escaped me today and I feel set free to this beautiful calm space," I softly reply.

I feel like I'm at the centre of a silent library, even though I am enclosed under a large green canopy outside. It is special for my mind to feel this still. It is a privilege to be the silent student. Like a sponge, I feel ready to soak up new knowledge. Today I'm glad to experience silence and stillness.

"Why is silence, noble silence, so important?" I ask.

"Firstly it is a mark of the respect of speaking only when spoken to. At first glance, the 'chatterbox' may appear to have the greatest knowledge, but it is the observers, the silent students who give their full attention. If you are talking, you cannot listen. You can only learn when you are silent, with full focus on your teacher," Pagoda explains.

I think about the many seminars or classes I've attended. I thought my intelligence was displayed by speaking up. I think of the questions fighting with each another in my head, preventing me from just listening and retaining what I was taught.

My lesson today is layered. I realise that it is respectful to wait until I'm spoken to. Only once conversation has been opened, can I respond with clear thought. Then it's the silence that invites a new-found clarity.

"Thank you." I am grateful for today's simple lesson. But is it simple? I ask myself. Years ago it took four days of focus on my own breath to silence my monkey-mind while learning Vipassana. That wasn't simple or easy. I wonder why I find it easy now sitting by my friend, instantly achieving the same result. This makes me remember how a tree can instantly change the way I am.

My friend Pagoda has cleared my thoughts and stilled my mind. I am calm, focussed and ready for more.

CHAPTER 3

Reaction

When I walk toward my friend I pass by the other nine large Pagoda trees. There are two other courtyards with four in each. In this final courtyard stands my friend, along with three others – twelve in total. When I first entered this area each tree excited me, yet I was drawn to connect fully to this one at whose side I now sit. I am unsure why I chose this tree, other than because his trunk is bigger, much bigger than the others. Was I drawn to her, thinking she was older and perhaps wiser?

I wait now beside my new friend. I wait until I'm spoken to. I intuitively understand the way I can show respect.

"Today I want to talk of reaction," Pagoda finally speaks.

I know that there are two ways to be: either

active or reactive. In a reactive state I am always controlled by events around me. Reactiveness is usually instant; there is never the time to consider first. This response usually comes from a sense of lack or the need to defend myself.

"Know that if you are reacting, you are feeding the fire of another. Some people only act out to get fuel back," Pagoda tells me.

My own life has been a great example of this. Only yesterday, I fell in love with something bright and colourful in a shop and bargained for it. Negotiations went in my favour, but then Michael walked up to me and told me I had a shopping addiction. He cautioned me to not purchase the item. I always love to bring back a little 'something' when I travel, as a reminder of the way a place makes me feel. I struggled with Michael's request. The item was not expensive and, besides, I had already paid for it – I was just waiting for it to be wrapped. I loved what I'd bought and Michael's caution only fired up my determination. My reaction was important.

Back on the bus I sat beside Michael, who was really annoyed. His energy was retracted and he avoided me for the next couple of hours. Our next tourist destination was the site of the terra cotta warriors. I walked through the big buildings alone. A current battle was being played out between Michael and me.

Back in Old China, civilization did as it was told. Many reactive thoughts came to my mind before I decide to let them go. I decided I didn't need to respond – I didn't have to fuel Michael's annoyance any further. I understood he had every right to be annoyed. He didn't love my souvenir. I knew his reaction was fuelled from not wanting to spend money just for the sake of it. It could have blown up into a battle of wills. Instead, I simply released my own feelings about it. Without a word, I allowed everything to return to a state of calm.

"Yesterday when I purchased a keepsake, Michael was annoyed. I could have reacted to his annoyance but I didn't," I say finally.

"Did you feel disempowered by your silence or empowered?" Pagoda asks.

"Strangely, I felt empowered by not being dragged into the drama. I accepted that Michael was annoyed. I also know it's how Michael feels sometimes when I buy things," I reply.

The question comes again: "Did you feel

empowered by your conscious lack of reaction?"

"Yes." I repeat the answer my teacher is seeking.

"This skill of being silent and composed and not reactive is important," Pagoda tells me.

After a moment of quiet reflection I ask, "Why?"

Before my teacher responds my memory takes me back to a fight that broke out a couple of days ago on our bullet train as we travelled between cities. It was entertaining as two men were yelling and arguing with one another. In the end, the more vocal of the men lost out. It appears both men wanted the same seat, but because they only spoke Chinese I could only piece the story together. In the end, one man retained dignity – he didn't yell or react. On the other hand, the other man was angry and out of control. He indicated that he wanted a fist-fight by punching one hand into the other. The silent man held his ground, and in the end he was awarded the seat they both wanted.

"My question is answered by a battle on the train a couple of days ago. The winner was the composed and silent one," I say aloud.

"Please take the opportunity to practise,"

Pagoda suggests.

I smile and nod.

I sit and contemplate the power of silence and quietly allowing others to experience things for themselves. I sense that this is going to set me free from the need to engage in conflict. I imagine how different my life would have been if I'd realised the importance of this sooner. There have already been 50 years of reactiveness. I make a conscious effort and promise to not be reactive in the future, instead embracing calmness by allowing conflict to simply fizzle out without me adding fuel to amplify the tension.

CHAPTER 4

Give-Away 'Essence'

This morning I remember a conversation I had with our guide when I asked if there was an ancient tree here in Xi'an China. She told me about the Pagoda and instantly I knew I was being led toward a new friend. Usually I explain at length why I wanted to know about the trees in China. I would explain my book-writing and then, inevitably, feel misunderstood. Whenever this would happen, I would feel judged, which only reinforced my need to explain myself. However, this time my conversation with our guide wasn't fuelled by me needing her to know about or understand me.

When I sit by Pagoda now I recall how I have finally let go of the desire to explain myself.

"I hear your thoughts today," Pagoda interrupts my inner chatter.

"I would usually be compelled to share, but I'm often misunderstood," I confirm my thoughts aloud.

"Is your usual need to explain, in order to gain the acceptance of others?" Pagoda asks.

"Yes, it is." I know that I long to be accepted by others.

"Your mystery will attract acceptance, as it will spark their curiosity to know more. By telling too soon, you give up your essence and end up throwing away what they want." Pagoda's words shed new light.

I consider this. My Pagoda teacher is correct. I've met some really interesting people during my life. As soon as I've felt I've known everything about someone, they've lost their mystery and intrigue – I've felt there was nothing more to learn from them. In contrast, when I've met those who hold their secrets close, then it has become my mission to find out more. I also know that I find those who talk too much about themselves, boring and self-absorbed.

"If someone asks what I'm writing, do I tell them?" I ask this because I've been in this situation before and I feel I've completely failed in my attempts to explain.

"Give only a little. Only once you have completed something, can it be shared. Then, share it only with those who come, excited to hear – which is how you have come to hear me. You are ready to learn. Only explain to those who have come to you, not you to them," Pagoda tells me.

I am almost relieved at being given permission to not have to explain myself to someone who isn't open or ready to hear. Not everyone needs to know everything about me. I do not need to explain myself to everyone, just as I don't want to always know everything about others.

"I appreciate this permission. Thank you," I finally say.

I feel an instant sense of freedom. I understand that when someone asks me for more information they are more open and won't be as likely to misunderstand me.

I look forward to testing this lesson in my life.

I realise that as soon as I focus on my own need to explain or share, my essence is eliminated from interactions with others and I give them the power. Conversely, I draw in many people who want to spend time with me when I am not self-absorbed and focussed on my own story. I feel genuinely interested in the essence of my travelling group. This makes for a fun time, as I mix with many different people in the group. They have so much to share and I find I learn more from this new, open way of being.

CHAPTER 5

Family

Travelling around the many streets of Xi'an, both within the city wall where history is contained, and outside where the new high-rises try to touch the sky, I notice that beside the roadways many Pagoda trees are planted.

I imagine how beautiful this city will look when spring gifts bunches of flowers in full bloom. I envisage beautiful white flowers hanging in clumps. These white panicle flowers are up to 30cm long, with each single flower no longer than a centimetre. They remind me of the wisteria hanging from my back veranda at of our farm-home in Australia.

While we visit China, the Pagoda trees are full of green leaves as it's the middle of summer. These leaves are preparing to turn lighter in colour then drop to the ground when autumn arrives next month.

I imagine the city workers will be busy collecting the discarded leaves daily to uphold the spotless regime.

As I approach Pagoda, I sense a female energy today. She's already prepared for my question and speaks first.

"We are family – connecting all Pagoda together to magnify our dedication to the scholar here in Xi'an. Knowledge is everything."

"Thank you for confirming that," I say.

Then I ask for confirmation of something I have sensed from when I first met Pagoda: "There are times when I feel you are female and then male. Which are you?"

"You are correct. I am both female and male. They call me a hermaphrodite tree which means I have both male and female reproductive organs. I can reproduce alone," Pagoda answers.

I am fascinated by this tree having the ability to be both male and female. No wonder I've been confused by the energy I have felt around Pagoda.

"You are the biggest Pagoda tree I've seen here. At first I thought you were the great-grandmother, then the great-grandfather. Now I know you're both.

Are you the oldest here at the *Little Wild Goose Pagoda*?"

"There were four of us planted first. Years later the rest were planted from our seeds that sprouted our offspring," Pagoda explains.

"Truly, your offspring? I imagine you've been proud to watch their growth?" I ask.

A gust of warm air encircles all the trees in this area. I take that as a 'yes' from them all.

I think of all the parents who have been both mother and father to their young. All the roles of support-giving, discipline and love, filled by just one parent.

I reach out my hand and place it on her trunk while holding my other hand on my heart. I feel like one of her young, welcomed as family into this family grove.

As I sit in the enveloped calm, my mind travels to the many types of human families. I wonder what the word itself means. Family can be defined as a specific group of people including partners, children, parents, aunts, uncles, cousins and grandparents – a group of people with common ancestors. Family means a group of things that are similar. My friend Pagoda is with his family here, where he has been planted, and then out beyond his home-base, connected with the extended family of Pagoda trees growing across China and the rest of the world.

I understand that my own family is not just made up of the people who birthed me. My family extends to Michael, my sons and the extended family into which I married. My world-family has always included my beloved friends. Family can also include every human, just as Pagoda trees globally all belong to the one family.

My thoughts linger on all humans being part of my family. My care and love should also extend to the whole of humanity, globally. I find this notion overwhelming, but it is a lovely sentiment that expands my heart.

As I rest by my friend Pagoda today, my heart feels large, big enough to include all of my human family here on earth. I feel an enormous connection to all.

CHAPTER 6

Embrace Your Personal Story

I noticed when I first met Pagoda that part of his trunk was repaired and then supported after being burned by fire. The caretakers have built large supports to hold his heavy limbs. I'm guessing that if these limbs had been left to grow naturally, they may have snapped off or needed the support of new undergrowth, perhaps shot out by Pagoda himself.

"I notice that your trunk has been damaged. What happened?" I ask with concern.

"This area was alight many years ago and all the buildings burned to the ground. The trees are all that remained. A miracle, some would say, but it hasn't been without scars," Pagoda explains. I feel his pain.

"Is this where you were burnt from that fire?" I point to the burnt area on his trunk and feel a heart-wrenching tug as Pagoda remembers.

"Yes, for years my life was alone and silent. The monks stopped their visits and this place was never as special as it had been. Notice that any tree here that was burnt has a thicker trunk. We had to exert all our strength to heal our brokenness," Pagoda shares.

"I can relate to that. Having been broken in my own young life, it has taken me years of dedication to strengthen and heal. I wonder if I will ever feel stronger from my own experience," I ponder aloud.

"Look at my shape and form. Never will I be what I would have been. Instead I have a different shape from my family grove. I am unique, I have a story. Remember – with your own story, comes your own personal wisdom. Be proud of your scars," Pagoda says.

Then he asks, "This is the reason you chose me, isn't it?"

"Well, it was your unique appearance that intrigued me," I comment, then add, "I knew you held a story – and in that story, I receive your gift."

I smile.

"You are the same as me. Embrace yourself completely."

I look at the ground. Paving surrounds my teacher. He has had to overcome restrictions in order to grow over 20 meters. He is as wide as he is high. Nothing has stood in the way of his full possible growth. I notice his very wide, strong-looking trunk and imagine that he had to exert enormous effort to stay living and not give up. The growth of my friend has taken determination. He is unique.

I sense that today's gift is Pagoda's encouragement for me to honour my own scars and the strength and effort it has taken me to hang in there, to grow and thrive regardless of the adversity I've faced.

This gift is very special. I see a new side of myself as I look at his gnarled trunk. I will no longer complain about my wrinkles, bulgy bits and my way of thinking. It all makes me who I am.

CHAPTER 7

Clarity for More

My guide shares that her seven year old son attends school each day. It is her responsibility to check his homework each night. Even at seven years of age, he is given much work each day. Her son is then tested on this work the next day, and the school rings her if her son doesn't do well on the test.

I consider the enormous pressure this entails. Here in China, education and knowledge are considered of the utmost importance.

The Pagoda tree is dedicated. It has been named the 'tree of the scholar'. I wonder what he can tell me about this.

Today is warm, yet the clear blue sky I am used to seeing back home is different from the sky here. The sky in China always seems to be blanketed in a smog, low cloud cover or haze.

Today when I sit beside my teacher, anticipating my daily lesson, I look up through his canopy to try and see the sky.

"The sky hasn't been clear for a very long time here in Xi'an." As usual Pagoda speaks first, reading my mind.

"Is it always like this? Back home in Australia we often have a clear blue sky, but I notice that isn't very common here in China," I comment. "Occasionally back home there's cloud cover, but the clouds are white and fluffy – not a full haze like here."

Pagoda explains: "Here in China, pollution is bad. There are as many people in some individual cities in China as there are in the whole of your huge country. Beijing is home to 24 million people. The cars, manufacture and progress have come at a cost. Knowledge and education are the most important things – they encapsulate China's progress. But unfortunately the air and sky are the victims of the pollution that comes with such progress."

"I was going to ask about the education here in China, and I would like to know why you are called the 'tree of the scholar'," I ask.

"You will see many of my species, not just here in Xian – I'm planted in every capital city throughout China. I bring the good fortune of clear thought, so people's minds can be filled with more information. It is believed that the most successful person is the one with knowledge. Education should never be taken for granted. It is the one thing that can never be taken away from someone. The only thief of knowledge is dementia," Pagoda shares.

I think how, back home, classrooms are considered boring by so many young students. Children complain that learning is boring, and they often don't pay much attention. The privilege of attending school has been forgotten and is no longer appreciated.

"I personally love to learn, but I know that not everyone has this same desire," I say genuinely.

"When locals visit here and sit beside me, I feel their dedication to expand their mind. I clear a space for them to then retain more knowledge. I also give them a sense of peace. Sometimes the pressure placed by Chinese parents on their young causes them stress. Smaller families place even more pressure on their children. It is an important goal to be the best and to give of their best always," Pagoda tells me.

"It is so different back at home in Australia. It is more accepted if someone is either academic or not. Only some people place strong academic pressure on their children."

I speak from my own personal experience on this. Then, changing the subject slightly I ask, "What would you say is the one thing that creates sadness here for people?"

I expect that Pagoda to answer that sadness is caused by being pushed to work and study harder. But his words surprise me.

"It isn't as you think. The push and ambition for more knowledge and learning is an honour. Sadness is not in people's minds; only sometimes in their hearts. Heads are full but hearts are sad when people find themselves alone, without anyone with whom to share their life. The population explosion hasn't happened in equal proportion. There are more boys than girls here in China."

"I think it's like this all over the world. Is there anything else you can tell me about the importance of learning?" I change the subject to bring the conversation back to the subject of learning. I am hoping for something profound.

"Every day you will learn something new. Honour that learning by holding onto it. Never discard knowledge as unimportant. However, the mind isn't more important than the heart. The heart is just as important. Your thoughts should be honoured and respected, but so should your feelings and emotions. I know that for a long time you have worked on your broken heart. It is now open and learning daily. Now is the time to give attention back to your thoughts. Release the negative thoughts and make room for good ones. Sitting here by me, I will make space for more clarity in your mind. "

The Pagoda challenges me: "Now go and learn, seek new knowledge and fill up on positive thoughts. Your mind is unique to you. What do you think?"

"At times I think too much. I over-analyse situations, obsessing over my past or feeling anxious about my future. I try to retain knowledge, but I do struggle with being a little foggy, like your sky here in China."

I look up again. Yes, that's exactly how it is.

"Close your eyes and imagine the sky without any clouds," Pagoda tells me. "It's clear and vibrant.

Even at night imagine a sky full of glistening stars. At the start and end of each day, with your eyes closed, watch the sky until it becomes clear. Your mind will also clear just by doing this. When you are back home in Australia, you don't have to close your eyes to imagine a clear sky. I want you to look up and focus on the clear vastness, taking your mind into this same place. Only when your thoughts are clear will you be ready to start a new day, or to close a day that has come to an end. You can also do this midway through your day by looking up. Go outside and just look up," Pagoda advises.

I felt sad that people here long for a blue sky.

I promise to do as Pagoda suggests when my own thoughts begin to cloud. The clear sky will become my metaphor for clear thought.

"Thank you."

My gift and lesson today have been to clear my mind so it can retain more – the gift of clarity.

CHAPTER 8

Control

As I lean into Pagoda, a question arises in me that I feel I can only whisper. I have heard that knowledge of some things isn't permitted freely here in China. For instance, searching for some topics on the internet is forbidden. I have heard that the Chinese revolution has been withheld from the younger generations. In 1989, many thousands of students went to Tiananmen Square to protest, and it is said that this resulted in civilian deaths in the thousands. The students had called for democracy, greater accountability, freedom of the press and freedom of speech. At the height of these protests, about 1 million people assembled in the Square. The troops supressed the protestors by firing at demonstrators with automatic weapons, killing the crowds and leading to mass civil unrest. Those in charge then began to restrict future learning about this, teaching only what they wanted the people to know.

I lean into Pagoda and wait patiently, my thoughts wandering on this topic. Back at home we have the freedom to learn about anything by searching for information on the worldwide web – but not here in China. Available content is restricted and blocked on computers through filters that only allow people to search on certain subjects.

"Deep in thought, I hear your mind," Pagoda whispers.

"Yes, I am bursting with questions today," I say. "I'm surprised to learn of the revolution and the death of so many young students back in 1989. I was about 20 years old then. It could have been me."

I imagine the devastation of losing so many of my own generation.

"Knowledge is good, it is power. But for those in power, others having knowledge also constitutes a threat. It wasn't just the young students. Many people – thousands of them – came to protest. Open fire of machine guns wounded and killed, and control was then restored as fear was embedded into people's souls. Such defeat was a way of teaching people that it isn't worth them speaking out against things with which they disagreed. People didn't stop thinking, but they stopped speaking about their thoughts. Before too long came the indoctrination of people to only think the way others wanted them to. They lost their freedom of opinion; they were stripped of the freedom to express."

As Pagoda tells me of the shift in how the people of China were instructed to live, I become sad. The only parallel I can find in my own life is when I was abused by my father as a child. I experienced a condition of mind control called 'gas-lighting', which is where someone is told that things didn't happen as they remembered them happening. History and reality were constantly being rewritten. If I dared to speak up, I was told that my thoughts were wrong. It was very confusing until eventually I gave up, having learned not to trust my own thoughts. My mind was under the control of another. Doubt fed uncertainty and, before I knew it, I had unlearned the ability to trust my own decisions. I formed the habit of always checking on others' opinions before consulting my own. It has taken me a long time to reverse this hard-learned lesson.

"What was it like before 1989, compared with afterwards?" I ask Pagoda.

"Before that time, a dream was etched into the minds of many. People always yearned and wanted more. The possibilities were endless," Pagoda says wistfully. I can sense the sadness in her tone.

She continues: "After the revolution, people stopped wanting and asking for more. Just like your own childhood experience of being controlled; you too stopped asking questions. You trusted your role models, your parents, to make decisions for you. The people in China did as they were told also. The threat of a loss of life was very real. Institutions like schools, intended to support learning and increase knowledge, became instruments of control also," Pagoda shares.

"Yes, knowledge is power – for good or ill. I'd never realised that today, right now, this very fact is being exploited."

I look up. The sky is clearer today. I can actually see a hint of blue. Ah, clarity!

After spending time with Pagoda today, I know that I must never waste an opportunity for knowledge. I must not take for granted the ability to learn about anything I wish. Today's lesson is about control and learning.

I feel a new sense of gratitude for all the opportunities for learning within my own life.

CHAPTER 9

Balance

Yin and yang, the balance of feminine and masculine, is also hidden deep within the Chinese culture of *Feng Shui*. This is the art of bringing balance to the home, office or any other building. The elements of metal, wood, water, air and fire all work together to create a harmonious life.

Years ago, when we built our farmhouse, I had a *Feng Shui* master map done of our home. A Bagua compass showed where more of a particular element was needed to bring balance in our home. The colours on our walls and placement of furniture were guided by this energetic map. I found this tradition and culture fascinating and I gave it my respect and attention. My home is balanced.

You only need to spend a night at our farm and you will announce by morning it's the best night's sleep you've ever had.

I have wondered while I've been visiting China about *Feng Shui*'s origins and what was behind the tradition.

Today we are very lucky – miraculously, the sky is vibrant blue. The sun shines brightly.

Beside my teacher Pagoda, I wait as usual to be spoken to first.

"Morning," Pagoda greets me.

"I have so many questions about the way *Feng Shui* brings balance, good fortune and health to the occupants of a home, or even to a building set out by drawing on its wisdom," I say.

"History. Originating in China almost 6,000 years ago, *Feng Shui*, also referred to as 'Geomancy', literally means 'wind' (Feng) and 'water' (Shui). It is an ancient method of constructing and optimising residences and businesses to bring about happiness, abundance and harmony," Pagoda begins to explain. "You have some knowledge of the outer world where balance can be achieved by creating order with the elements. It is time now to look within. Chinese medicine is a method of looking at organs and their functions, just like rooms within a house."

"I have used Chinese medicine at different times in my life. My body absorbs these well and balance is eventually restored," I agree with where my teacher is leading me today.

"You have neglected some of your internal rooms. You have overloaded some rooms and in others, you are empty. The five elements correspond to your organs and rooms," Pagoda continues.

I nod. I know this is true. I have put myself last for quite some time. (Who am I kidding? I've put myself last forever.) I hate putting people out by requesting something special to eat. I have learned to just put up with pain, ignoring it and hoping for everything to miraculously heal.

"Emotions connect to your physical body and, over time, permanent damage has been done."

I immediately think of the inflammatory disorder in my joints, which flares up when I eat the wrong things.

"Do you have any wisdom about my lack of inner harmony?" I ask.

"You need to give your inner home a clean, then

bring in items like in *Feng Shui*, just as though your body were a physical building. Nourish yourself with every bite of food and be quenched with herbal teas. You will very soon experience balance and harmony inside and out, which will lead to longevity."

I sit for a while in a position of mediation. My legs are crossed in front of me and my hands rest gently on my knees. I know that I really need to commit to this if the aches and pains are going to leave my body.

In the distance I observe a Thai Chi class. Fluid smooth movements are made by very old people. They are nimble and flexible. This is something worth aspiring to be.

I'm motivated to restore balance within.

CHAPTER 10

State of Mind

As I walk up to Pagoda, he wastes no time in beginning today's lesson.

"Just as the mind can be your best friend, it can also be your enemy. How often does a nagging thought wreck your day?" Pagoda asks me.

I understand this is true when my own thoughts repeat themselves. Over and over, the same thought ends up convincing me I'm not pretty or good enough. At times I think I'm not smart enough and I avoid putting myself forward in fear that I am wrong.

"There is such a fear of standing out as the one who has it wrong," I finally say.

"But what if you are right?" Pagoda asks. "What if your obsessed mind-chatter is wrong? You are only in a mess if your thoughts are tangled without the clarity of truth."

Though I know this is true, it is still easier sometimes to not say things. When I've obsessed over a self-destructive thought, clarity is the furthest thing from my mind.

"How do I know when to trust my own thoughts? How do I know when the truth is being echoed through my mind?" I ask.

"Obsessive negative insecurity always involves comparing yourself with others. If you think you are not enough, it's because you see someone whom you perceive as more beautiful or smart. Please stop making these comparisons," Pagoda requests.

"I don't do this as often these days," I respond.

"What about your weight? Don't you feel less beautiful because you carry some excess weight?"

I nod. I do feel judged by others because of this.

"Your teachers are the food and clothing companies that want you to spend your money on becoming the opposite of what you are. During the Renaissance, you would have been considered very beautiful with your voluptuous curves. If you are naturally fair-skinned, big brand companies encourage you to use products for tanned brown skin. And if you had darker skin, they would try to sell you skin-lightening creams. The self-doubt stems from the belief that you need to be different. It is a powerful person who is happy with who they are. You need confidence to simply be who you are. You need to silence any self-talk that puts you down in any way," Pagoda states.

He is right. Sometimes I'm not worried at all about this. Then an odd comment catches me and sets off my insecurities. My obsessive thoughts are fuelled by not accepting myself and living today exactly as I am.

"What do you suggest I do to clear my negative thoughts?" I ask.

"Close your eyes to look inside the core of yourself. Send a smile throughout your body. In your mind, see calm. In your feet, see strength. Then up through your body to your head, watch closely to replace any negative thought with a positive one," Pagoda offers.

I stare at my feet, visualising them relaxing. Then I focus on each body part, watching it relax. Any pain caught throughout my body is released, so that I am calm. I experience a sense of freedom from my obsessive thoughts, instead feeling calm, exactly as I am. I don't focus on what I could be, but instead simply experience myself as curvy. I see poor health replaced by fitness. In my mind I see what is beneath and possible.

I have enjoyed my inner vision being stirred today, and I look forward to paying more attention to how I feel about my body and examining where those thoughts come from.

CHAPTER 11

My Journey Continues

Leaving the bustling city of Xian, I head to Beijing, a city with the same population as the whole country of Australia. We take a rickshaw through the back streets of Old Beijing. Walking and climbing along the Great Wall of China is a massive highlight of my trip. Finally, we experience abundant clear blue skies.

The Great Wall of China has a long history. It winds its way along, seemingly forever. I watch as the occasional butterfly dances around and past me as I witness one of the Wonders of the World.

My mind is clear, calm and present. For several days now, I have experienced this calm silent mind. It's been a refreshing way to experience the many villages and old Chinese gardens throughout Beijing and Shanghai.

I am surrounded by people, yet I don't feel overwhelmed. I find myself going with the flow. I take in all the sights without feeling like I need to be anywhere else.

I know that my new friend Pagoda has given me her/his gift of clarity, calm and focus. These things are needed for my mind to be open for further learning.

The scholar is ready, and the teacher shows up. My teacher Pagoda has shown me the importance of clearing my cluttered mind. I have learned that it isn't only important for my external world to be calm and balanced – it is also important for my inner world, my physical body and mind, to be restored to a space of balance… my own Yin and Yang.

After seeing a Doctor of Chinese Medicine about the inflammation in my joints and organs, these are being addressed. My digestion is linked, as well as my liver. The liquid in my body has not been eliminated, which is causing the inflammation. I agree to try some herbs.

In no hurry to go anywhere, I am open to experiencing the outside busyness of the cities, while my own inner state is calm.

The cities of Northern and Central China have held a focus on learning. The scholar is valued and admired for her dedication.

The Pagoda has restored calm and peace of mind in me and, most importantly, clarity and focus.

My new focus on living in the present moment has been enriched by the culture of China.

I visualise myself one last time while still in China, resting my back against Pagoda.

"Is your name Li?" I am the first to speak, interested to see whether my hunch is correct.

"Yes my name is Li. The meaning of 'Li' is 'pretty and powerful'. The origin of the name Li is Chinese. If used for a female it means 'pretty' and for a male it means 'powerful'."

This sums up my whole encounter with Pagoda. It has all been Pretty Powerful.

I hold my hand against the trunk of Pagoda. I feel deeply, I see lovingly and I am calm, so very still and centred. My focus is on creating a balanced, happy and healthy life.

I promise to share the gifts of Li Pagoda. I know

that these lessons are not just for me.

"Thank you," I say to my teacher.

"Thank you... now go and encourage a clear mind and the importance of learning more," Pagoda rustles his large canopy of green leaves.

I feel humbled, enriched and calm.

Also by Rochelle

Banyan Tree Wisdom: My Gift to You
Banyan Tree Wisdom: Wisdom Cards
Meeting Rosie Banyan:
Learning Forgiveness, Trust and Love
I Give You My Word: Journal

EARTH GIANT TREE GIFT SERIES
(GIFT BOOKS & AUDIO BOOKS)

Book 1: Oak Tree's Gift
Book 2: Baobab Tree's Gift
Book 3: Banyan Tree's Gift
Book 4: Rainbow Gum's Gift
Book 5: Olive Tree's Gift
Book 6: Pagoda Tree's Gift
Book 7: Snow Gum Tree's Gift
Book 8: Moreton Bay Fig's Gift

ALCHEMY OILS

Banyan Tree: 'Restore Balance', 'Dream',
'Release' & 'Beauty Wisdom Power'
Oak Tree: 'Truth'
Baobab Tree 'Connection'
Banyan Tree 'Balance'
Rainbow Gum 'Joy'
Olive Tree 'Confidence'
Pagoda Tree 'Clarity'
Snow Gum Tree 'Motivated'
Moreton Bay Fig 'Dreaming'

www.treevoice.global

About the Author

A busy business owner, wife and mother, Rochelle thrived in the corporate and finance world in her early adult years. Then, after her fourth son, a wave of post-natal depression debilitated her, forcing her to re-visit the horrors of her sexually abusive childhood. With grit and determination she laboured against her own broken past and breathed life back into her shutdown heart, cracking open its language and capturing it in writing. She learned to trust in the universal soul path she'd stepped onto.

Each time she experienced a healing method that helped her, Rochelle became qualified in that field to then help others. She became a Bowen Therapist, Reiki and Seichem Master, Clinical Hypnotherapist using NLP methods, Journey Worker and Intuitive Healer. She also owned and ran a Day Spa and Healing Centre in North East Victoria.

Rochelle now immerses herself in connections with nature as they flow, bringing to life the lessons and messages through writing, speaking and facilitating. Her journey has led her to many parts of the globe. She has pitched to Hollywood in New York; she has hosted women's retreats in Bali; she has learned from poverty-stricken leaders in Senegal Africa; and she discovered the 'simple' life in Vanuatu.

Rochelle's message is honest, raw and authentic, and her words are greatly needed as we all navigate our next chapter here on earth.

AUTHOR, SPEAKER, ALCHEMIST,
A LOVER OF NATURE AND
VIBRANT LIVING

Connect with Rochelle

hello@treevoice.global

www.facebook.com/TreeVoiceAuthor

www.facebook.com/RochelleHeverenAuthor

Instagram: @treevoiceglobal

Instagram: @rochelle_with_love_x

www.treevoice.global

www.ingramcontent.com/pod-product-compliance
Lightning Source LLC
Chambersburg PA
CBHW032050290426
44110CB00012B/1032